Talking About
Death and
Bereavement
in School

of related interest

Children Also Grieve
Talking about Death and Healing
Linda Goldman
ISBN 978 1 843 10 808 5

**Talking with Children and Young
People about Death and Dying**
2nd edition
Mary Turner
Illustrated by Bob Thomas
ISBN 978 1 843 10 441 4

Grief in Young Children
A Handbook for Adults
Atle Dyregrov
Foreword by Professor William Yule
ISBN 978 1 843 10 650 0

Grief in Children
A Handbook for Adults
2nd edition
Atle Dyregrov
Foreword by Professor William Yule
ISBN 978 1 843 10 612 8

Lost for Words
Loss and Bereavement Awareness Training
John Holland, Ruth Dance, Nic Macmanus and Carole Stitt
ISBN 978 1 843 10 324 0

Great Answers to Difficult Questions about Death
What Children Need to Know
Linda Goldman
ISBN 978 1 84905 805 6

Good Grief 1
Exploring Feelings, Loss and Death with Under Elevens
2nd Edition
Barbara Ward and Associates
ISBN 978 1 85302 324 8

Interventions With Bereaved Children
Susan C Smith and Sister Margaret Pennells
ISBN 978 1 85302 285 2

Talking About Death and Bereavement in School

How to Help Children Aged 4 to 11 to Feel Supported and Understood

Ann Chadwick

Jessica Kingsley *Publishers*
London and Philadelphia

Illustrations throughout the book kindly provided by Rosemary Asplin.

First published in 2012
by Jessica Kingsley Publishers
116 Pentonville Road
London N1 9JB, UK
and
400 Market Street, Suite 400
Philadelphia, PA 19106, USA

www.jkp.com

Library of Congress Cataloging in Publication Data
Chadwick, Ann, 1937-
  Talking about death and bereavement in school
: how to help children aged 4
to 11 to feel supported and understood / Ann Chadwick.
    p. cm.
  ISBN 978-1-84905-246-7 (alk. paper)
  1. Bereavement in children. 2. Death--Social aspects. 3. Death--
Psychological aspects. I. Title.
  BF723.G75C47 2012
  155.9'37083--dc23
                              2011025155

British Library Cataloguing in Publication Data
A CIP catalogue record for this book is available from the British Library

ISBN 978 1 84905 246 7
eISBN 978 0 85700 527 4

Printed and bound in Great Britain

Contents

Acknowledgements

Many friends have helped me through the computer complexities (with which I am much too old to learn how to grapple), while others have done the proof-reading and corrected my English. I am so grateful to them all (and we are still friends!).

My sister, Rosemary, has drawn the illustrations and my niece, Emily, has prepared the text for publication. Without them both this would not be in your hands now.

Preface

What can you, as a teacher or member of staff, do to help when bereavement hits your school? Perhaps it is a pupil or member of staff who dies, or it might be a child's friend or family member. School staff who find themselves in this predicament often don't know where to start.

Death is a taboo subject in Western society. Grief hurts, and sometimes teachers are so shocked and stunned by tragic events that it is difficult to continue with the everyday teaching role.

Children are probably totally unprepared for death, but they are resilient. A teacher can help them to face this event in their lives.

Death can provide a tremendous learning opportunity. As the poet John Donne wrote in 1624, 'Any man's death diminishes me.'[1] In that diminished place

---

1 Meditation 17, *Devotions upon Emergent Occasions*.

parents often expect the school to know what will help both themselves and their child. I trust that this book will assist you in this.

Whether you are a school teacher or a member of the support staff, this book is written for you. Often it is the playground helper or dinner lady who first picks up the news of a death. They may need help so that they can give meaningful responses to bereaved children, but nonetheless they are an important adjunct to the work done by teachers or counsellors.

With informed, wise staff the school can become the secure, nurturing environment the bereaved child needs, and at the same time provide a golden opportunity to add to pupils' understanding.

Note: To avoid over-use of gender pronouns, the author has used either gender when discussing children, teachers or staff, but the reader should assume inclusive language, as the whole text applies equally to males and females.

Society's attitude to death

Death is a taboo subject in society. Children who are caught up in the reality of it may experience half truths, be shut out from discussions or even be scolded for showing feelings. Is it any wonder that they often have a garbled version of what has really happened? They need to understand that giving expression to grief is both normal and healthy.

Bereavement is the biggest thing that can ever happen to a person. Grief is the price we pay for love, and expressing that pain is the best way of growing through it.

Teaching opportunities

The event of bereavement in a school is a sad one, but it can also be turned into a positive learning experience by teaching children about death and grief.

Teaching opportunities vary with the age of the child concerned.

Children aged 4 to 7

For very young children in infant school or kindergarten, teaching about death is best done in context, by correcting wrong perceptions.

One 4-year-old dying in hospital cheerfully said, 'I know what happens when you die. Sister flushes you down the toilet.' He had seen his tropical fish disposed of in this way. It presented a chance to correct his perception. Four days later he was in his coffin, but by bringing up the subject he had shown that he was ready for some relevant facts.

Take time in class to discuss the difference between live and dead flowers. Different species have certain lifespans – poppies die in a day while chrysanthemums might last two weeks.

It is important to acknowledge the death of a school pet, such as a guinea pig, rather than buying a replacement. This serves three purposes:

1. *It provides an opportunity for change.* The school can decide whether to continue keeping animals.

2. *It validates tears,* exposing children to the sadness of loss and the appearance of death. When alive, the animal was warm and active. In death, it is cold and unattractive. As with a bone from the butcher that a dog has discarded, dead things become smelly and must be disposed of. Children need to know that sadness and tears are acceptable. An important lesson is to help them to accept that death hurts since it is the price we pay for love. Big boys (and girls) do cry!

3. *It provides a chance to discuss the rites of passage of the dead.* Children may well want some form of burial service for the guinea pig. This is welcome, and it can have surprisingly beneficial results.

Children aged 7 to 11

By the age of 7, children in primary or elementary school know the difference between the concrete and the ephemeral.

They can grasp the concept of 'never returning' and can see some of the social consequences of a death in a family. Sadly, families can give conflicting pictures of how to view death:

An 8-year-old picks up a dead hedgehog: 'Don't touch that – it's dead,' says the parent.

The parent says, 'Heaven's a happy place where Granny's at peace.' *The child thinks, 'So why is everyone crying so much?'*

The parent explains, 'God wanted Daddy to live in Heaven with Him so He came and took him.' *The child thinks, 'Why should God have him? I wanted Daddy to live here with us.'*

The parent says, 'We had to have the cat put to sleep.' Grandad's grave reads, 'Fallen asleep in the arms of Jesus.' *The child thinks, 'I'm too scared to go to sleep in case I die like them. Anyway, what does Mummy mean when she shouts, "You children go to sleep at once"?'*

Perhaps unkindest of all, and one that affects people for years to come: the parent says, 'Don't cry. You're the man of the house now that Daddy's dead.' *The child thinks, 'I'm 9 and I've got to look after Mummy. What does that mean? Drive the car? Go out to work? Climb ladders? Paint the house?'*

Death and decay are subjects that aren't normally talked about, but children often have questions about them, and will want to know the answers.

Permit healthy questioning, such as, 'Do worms come and eat you up?' Don't side-step any chances to teach the facts about death.

Let us look at death and grief in more depth. It is not a subject children are encouraged to address until it hits them, and when it does families want things tidied away as quickly as possible. I'm suggesting that we put the subject on the curriculum, teaching it alongside the facts of life! Families, friends and teachers give conflicting pictures of how to view death.

I believe that it is your responsibility as teachers and school staff members to correct and, if necessary, refute the information and instructions given to children in the kind of statements listed above.

Children aged 7 and above are of an age when they can question, and you are in a powerful role to influence them. While this should not be abused, you can play an essential role in educating children facing death so that they do not perpetuate the nonsensical remarks of the generation before them.

At this age children have an inquisitive nature. They may well have studied simple pumping systems and related that to the heart and the blood supply, and will rightly question what happens when the heart stops. Death ensues.

In context, it's quite appropriate to examine live and dead objects and note the difference. For example, some children might walk to school past the local abattoir, others via a pets' cemetery, while others may have seen a dead lamb on a farm or a dead squirrel in the road. Most will know someone whose cat or dog has died and will have been told a variety of traditional stories and folklore.

Heaven or...?

By its very nature, death stirs up a spiritual awareness and provides an important opportunity to teach children about beliefs.

There is a true story about three children aged 4 to 9 who decided to have a funeral for a recently deceased squirrel. They had a procession, carrying the corpse in a shoebox, the youngest bearing some withered daisies. The 7-year-old clasped an old dictionary in place of a prayer book because it had 'gold squirly writing on it'.

They closed their eyes while the eldest intoned, 'In the name of the Father, and of the Son and in-the-hole-he-goes.' With that the box lid was whisked off and the squirrel deftly shot into the prepared grave. The parents, who had to hide their amusement, admitted that the Holy Ghost had now taken on a whole new meaning for them!

Where do children learn about processions, solemnity, flowers on graves and special prayers to God? They view them on the TV news, see a hearse or drive past a cemetery. What they need is reinforcement for the facts they have right and amendment for those they are muddled about.

In the face of death, even a child with no religious upbringing will usually at some point be confronted with religious words, such as, 'Granny has gone to Heaven' (as opposed to on holiday) or 'Jesus came and took her.'

In an interfaith school, teachers have a responsibility to address the child's spiritual understanding by at least directing him or her to people who can give an explanation. Teachers can explain their own belief systems to children, pointing out that there are alternative belief systems and that these will be part of the child's future discovery.

In a school that is quasi-Christian, it is easy to talk about Heaven and to give facts about Jesus by drawing on the Christmas and Easter stories. Where other faiths are represented, the relevant perspectives of death should also be explored.

School children are at an age when they can begin to understand the concept of the soul as distinct from the body. I am a Christian and I use the term 'the special person that they were' to illustrate to a 10-year-old what 'soul' means to me.

My niece knows that Grandma's body has been burnt, her ashes buried and her special belongings distributed to those she loved, but the person who was Grandma lives on in our memories. We still refer to things she would have said or done, the shape of her arms and lap and the memories of being read to – they are all part of Grandma which remains for us.

In my own family, we believe we will be reunited in Heaven. Most religions believe that there is a part of us which lives on after death, but this belief has different forms. The idea of a person living on in memories applies to all, whether religious or secular.

The most tangible example of death leading to new life is the autumn leaf, which, having died and fallen, is then transformed into compost to enable the tree to go on living.

Death and decay are not subjects that are frequently talked about, but they will be present in children's minds. I urge you to be brave and allow discussion. Be clear about where the physical stops and belief begins; permit healthy questions. Yes, the worms do come and eat you up: these are the facts of death and you have a responsibility to teach them.

At the age of 11, children may realize that they have been fed a number of traditional 'stories' about the facts of life. Few 11-year-olds still think that babies are found under gooseberry bushes, but what opportunity do they get to disprove the tales of death, when some adults refuse to believe that Elvis Presley is dead and others have themselves frozen in ice for a couple of generations? The concept of sitting on a cloud playing a harp or becoming a twinkling star needs to be consigned to the gooseberry bushes and children must be taught how to examine what is written about belief systems to help clear their thinking.

Your educative role is, I hope, now clear to see, but there is one further area which only you can really tackle – namely, society's reaction to death. If children are caught up in it for real, they will experience half-truths, be left out and told to behave as normal. They may be discouraged or even scolded for showing their feelings and witness some strange and clandestine behaviour from adults, such as being told that the dead person will come back to sit by their bed at night to make sure they have nice dreams. Children are unlikely to receive a straightforward role model from their parents, and if they do, they will be confused, as the world around will probably not approve of the parents' actions, such as taking children to see the dead body or to attend the funeral.

Concepts of death

In recent years teachers have become much better at explaining the facts of life, so why not the facts of death too?

The problem is, we adults often don't know what we believe ourselves. One thing we do know, unlike the young children in our care, is that death is irreversible.

Children know that a lost toy can be found during a spring clean. A distant auntie comes to stay, then disappears, but still sends birthday cards. An empty guinea pig cage may soon be filled again.

It is hard for a child under 6 to comprehend that dead means gone forever. After all, TV bad guys, such as those in the Tom and Jerry cartoons, sustain total mutilation, yet live for next week's episode. Never in a TV cartoon are the dead collected up, buried and mourned, leaving the aching hurt that the child is now experiencing.

In the case of children aged 7 to 11, they will rightly question what happens when the heart stops and death ensues. As they study history and read of kings being beheaded or Egyptians being mummified, they are ready for facts we might think are too gruesome for them. Their need to make sense of the facts of death provides a marvellous teaching opportunity.

Children of this age want facts. Dead objects don't need food, water or care. They also decay. Children know this from having kept tadpoles in a jam jar or having smelt the water in a vase of dead daffodils left in the classroom over half-term. What they also need to know is, 'Does *everything* decay? And where does Heaven (or new life) fit into all this?'

Death brings grief that, in turn, brings strange and uncontrollable, erratic emotions. Children need to be taught that expressing grief is both healthy and normal, as our society often says the opposite. Help them contrast the Indian or Iranian crowd they may see on TV – deeply wailing men and women – with the stiff self-control usually observed in many Western societies. Ask them which reaction they feel is best – if they had to keep a really strong feeling inside, what would it do to them?

What have they gleaned so far in their young lives about crying? On the whole they will have learnt that it is weak or infantile, that they 'shouldn't do it'. However, keeping grief inside eats away at us, and some cultures are much better at letting it out than others.

To convey this to children you will also have to re-educate yourself and look at your own response system. To weep with a little one who comes to tell you his big sister has just died shows that you really care that he is hurting. The child discovers that adults feel pain and all this striving to keep a 'stiff upper lip' puts a barrier up just when the grief-stricken person most needs to feel the touch of human kindness. Of the professionals who worked with me in a children's hospital, it was those that wept with families when a child died who were felt to be the ones who really cared and understood.

Effects on the school

When a staff member or pupil dies, the whole school is affected. How should the children be told? Should the parents be informed first by letter or should an announcement be made in assembly?

Each school will need to decide what response to take. Indeed, governors or school leaders are well advised to draw up a policy and make it known to staff before the need to implement it arises.

In a situation where it is known that a staff member or child will die in the near future, there needs to be some forward planning to determine how the news will be handled when the time comes.

It is also important to consider when the collective grieving ritual is complete, so that the school can begin to return to normal. In fact, there is no 'normal' – there is simply a new state in which all have shared in the same hurt and that may well have deepened relationships in the school.

For children, the experience will have forced them to acknowledge that death isn't just reserved for old people. If a child has been killed crossing the road or died having a minor operation, it may well shake children's sense of security, causing them to want to explore their own mortality.

In such a situation it is quite appropriate to have class discussions with the children about things like whether they want to be buried or cremated, or whether they would want their mountain bike given to a child who has nothing, or just left for their little brother who already has one.

Not long ago a school mini-bus crashed, killing two teachers and a number of pupils. Parents flocked to the school, not knowing if their child was alive or dead. The press wanted their news stories and pictures; staff and governors were shaken to the core after losing colleagues and children and anxious about their collective responsibility in the matter.

Such a situation requires an established school policy which can be quickly put into operation when it is needed.

For example, one teacher might be assigned to deal with the press, another with the police and rescue services, while a third sets up a communication system with parents and another takes responsibility for how the children will be dealt with in the short term and helped in the immediate aftermath.

Clearly, these members of staff will need to co-operate with one another to ensure that the same, accurate information is being given out. This system can be applied whether there is a major school tragedy or a single death in traumatic circumstances.

As indicated earlier, the opportunities for discussions about afterlife will flow quite naturally from such an event. The school may have to face opposition from parents at being so open with young children about death, or perhaps suggesting that children attend or participate in the funeral. Providing that staff can instil confidence in parents that they are able to cope with children in grief, parents may allow the school to take the lead.

Of course it is imperative that parents who do not wish for their children to be involved in these discussions are accommodated.

So, what advice can I give you about coping with children in grief? Children operate in the here and now, so their anguish may soon be supplanted by other things, such as a missing lunch-box or the excitement of passing their cycling proficiency test. They need to be given permission to weep and an opportunity to make their unique contribution. Some may want to make cards, write poems or put together flower arrangements, others will be prepared to read at the funeral or to read a poem to the class which describes the personal events which surround the death. They, like adults, will want to do something, so decide together what will be done collectively and individually.

It is important to make sure the children's contribution is appropriate. Having lived close to Aberfan in Wales, where in 1966 a coal-tip slid into the school crushing 116 children, I was horrified to note that the nation's sympathy was expressed by sending, literally, train-loads of toys to the few remaining children. Sadly, they already had a plethora of toys from their dead friends – such action only goes to show how irrational many of our responses to death are.

Death of a staff member

Reaction of adults

Teachers and support staff will be shocked by the news that a staff member has passed away, even if the person has been ill. We adults have an inbuilt resistance to accepting death, especially that of someone our age or younger.

You may be inclined to limit your involvement on the grounds that you do not want to get in the way of the immediate family. You will also try not to be shocked or sad – you have a class waiting to be taught, and the show must go on! Yet it is worth grasping the educational opportunity by involving the children.

How should we tell them? How much do they need to know? What if we burst into tears? These are some of the natural misgivings that will be flying around the staffroom.

Some thought needs to be given to the pupils directly affected. The replacement staff member may be treated with anger. Anger is a natural stage in the grieving process. It will take a lot for the replacement person to acknowledge with the children that they would rather have their old teacher back, but it will be worth it.

It is often easier to tell the children the news all together. This task probably falls to the head teacher, but the head may appreciate another staff member offering to explain the contingency arrangements.

Adults in the school need to understand that other staff members are hurting and probably fearful of showing it to colleagues. A few hugs and spare tissues can be very meaningful. Tears, anger, disbelief and fear are natural accompaniments to grief, but they don't sit lightly on the shoulders of staff.

It is important that, rather than trying to carry on as if nothing has happened, the teacher acknowledges that the school family is hurting. Don't be afraid to show pupils that adults as well as children can hurt.

When support staff come across children who have been particularly affected by the death, they should try to encourage them to talk. A gentle 'You must be missing Miss Thomsett,' can give the child permission to open up about the subject; the flow of tears is very valuable.

Grief does not go away by suppressing it, but by expressing it. Parents will be far less likely to raise the subject and may just urge the child to 'get on with the new teacher'. Children will not be overwhelmed with grief for hours on end, they may not even weep, but they should be given the chance to say what they valued about that teacher and to raise questions about their understanding of death. It is worth the head teacher gathering all the staff together after a death, allowing the adults to express their feelings and encouraging them to open up the subject with the children.

We feel so guilty in our society when we cause someone to cry; if only we could learn that we have done them a service.

Reaction of pupils

Initially, especially with younger children, there may not be a pronounced reaction to a death. Infants may not see its relevance to them, but over the ensuing days they may feel the effect of its impact on other pupils. At this age they are essentially selfish. They may cry, not so much because Miss Thomsett has died, but because they had lent her their special Japanese doll in traditional costume and they fear that it won't be returned.

Those children directly affected may initially ask penetrating questions, but then show normal behaviour for a while. This is often misconstrued as the children having got over the death quickly or not really caring. The fact is that in a normal day the child is only aware of the death intermittently, whereas adults are preoccupied with the loss and unable to get on with their daily routine. Older children need to be given permission to cry and an opportunity to make their own unique contribution. So often they will feel they have to be grown up and not express their feelings – permission is a very potent thing when dealing with grief.

Death of a pupil

When a pupil dies, the affected class will grieve much longer than the rest of the school. Those who had a close friendship with the dead child will need some extra care.

If the child had a specified workspace, leave this empty and occasionally refer to it. This gives permission for grief to continue in the hearts and minds of the children. The dead child made a contribution to the class and continues to be part of it despite his death. Continue to refer to the dead child: 'Peter you go and sit in David's seat and work with Kirstie for a while.' The school holidays will be the natural time to allow for movement of furniture and for the empty space to be diminished, as the class will move on in time.

Multiple losses in the school

Where several children and teachers die in one accident, staff, parents, pupils, governors, statutory agencies and the press all become entwined. Areas of responsibility need to be clear. Senior staff and governors may deal with outside agencies but they also have a duty to other staff, children and parents. Information needs to be verified before being formally given. This is where the prepared policy can be quickly brought into use. It is useful to have a 'practice run' before the policy is approved so that any gaps can be identified. It is worth doing; do not be beguiled into thinking you will never need it!

Parts of the school may be set aside as spaces where grieving and sharing can take place, preferably with a coffee machine and counsellors on hand.

Up to at least a week after the funerals, each day could combine periods of normal working, time out for grieving, a formal remembrance and information time. Pupils will be grateful for a routine, even though they are preoccupied. They may want to cry, express their pain through drawing or go to the 'set apart' space. They will also need to know that they won't be told off for not completing their work.

There is a delicate balance between reacting to the shock and moving on. The most vulnerable are the junior members of staff, who are dealing directly with the children's questions and pain.

The anxiety/relief of survivors and their relatives is a real issue that needs talking through. Grieving parents may form support groups, while parents of survivors may feel isolated in their guilt. The school could offer a coffee evening to all parents to discuss how the bereavement is being dealt with. This could be coupled with planning a memorial. It would serve to bring bereaved and survivor parents face to face in controlled circumstances and help to relieve some of the awkwardness between the two groups. You need to allow time for informal talking and weeping to happen naturally.

How the school responds

Collectively

The response to a death could be minimal, with just a staff member attending the funeral. On the other hand, it could involve working with the children to write a letter of condolence, making cards and saying prayers, or even taking part in the funeral service. In the latter case, the family needs to be consulted because the combination of children and death is itself very emotional.

Generally, other than a loss in the immediate family, it is best for children to be given the choice about attending the funeral service. If children attend, having some parent helpers can relieve the stress on bereaved teachers. If it is a child who has died, staff need to be prepared for the extra shock of seeing a small coffin.

Children attending a funeral should be told clearly what will happen. Naturally, many will cry, but they should also be encouraged to say goodbye and to commit the person into God's care.

On returning to school they can do a special activity and be given a drink and biscuit as a treat. This allows those affected to come back out of their sadness and those not so affected to relax after the solemnity of the funeral.

Those who didn't attend can be involved in making a flower arrangement or picture to go into each classroom or the head teacher's office.

In these ways the school collectively acknowledges the death, admits that they are all in some way affected, and uses a variety of ways to show their sorrow and care. A suitable class outing could be to go to the cemetery a few days later and see the flowers. This could be combined with a learning project, such as looking at the kinds of trees growing there or the different types of writing on the headstones. The children could compare the sentiments of the Victorian tombstones with those of the modern ones. They could perhaps make up their own epitaphs too. There will always be the class joker though who will write:

Here lies Fred,
Now he's definitely dead,
I can have the roller-skates back!

Thinking about how they would like to be remembered can be quite salutary and working out how old they would want to be at the time of death can be quite a challenging exercise. A trip to the cemetery also gives scope for looking at the euphemisms which we use such as 'pushing up the daisies', 'kicking the bucket', 'popping one's clogs', 'six feet under', 'meeting one's maker', 'dead as a dodo', etc. It could even be fun!

Helping individuals

Some children may be more deeply affected by the death of a staff member or pupil than others. Try to determine why this is. A family member in hospital may have died recently. They may feel somehow responsible yet confused that their action or neglect has caused this degree of upset in the school.

Help them to explore their feelings and raise questions. They may be angry that classmates seem unaffected. Acknowledge that this is a legitimate feeling. Allow for their preoccupation and give them short tasks that fit their concentration span. Reinforce their security where you can.

It is easier for someone with a confused or frightened mind to work with a couple of friends on practical things than to deal with cognitive matters at the same speed as the rest of the class. Use the different levels of reaction to teach the class about depths of relationships. Encourage them to express friendship and concern for each other. Don't allow the fantasy that the dead person was perfect though.

Case study: Responding to the death of a child's mother

You are informed that 7-year-old Matthew is staying with Grandma while Mum is in hospital. Three days later you learn that Mum has died. Who needs to know? Should the children be told? If so, should just Matthew's classmates be told, or the whole school?

It is a good idea for the class teacher to visit the father at home to discuss how best to handle Matthew's return. Subject to the parent's wishes, it is useful to tell Matthew's class about his mother's death while he is away and to make a card to send to him.

All staff, including the school secretary and caretaker, need to know about the situation so they can express condolences to Matthew on his return. On the first few days back it may be helpful to involve him with adults and just one or two classmates. He will appreciate being special – but not singled out, which is different.

Help the class receive Matthew on his first day back. Link his return with other projects, such as the weather. 'Yesterday was wet and windy, and today the sun is out. Yesterday was a sad day for Matthew. Do you want to tell us what happened?' This may free him to talk about his mum's funeral or some other aspect of her death. Make sure you have your facts right though.

Use this opportunity to tell the class that Matthew will feel sad for a long time because he will be missing his mum. Be especially sensitive if the death occurs around Mother's Day or Easter.

Effects on adults

Other adults will tend to avoid Matthew in the same way they might avoid a bereaved neighbour. Encourage them instead to say how sorry they are and to ask about other relatives. It is helpful to reinforce for the child that it has really happened by making him aware that other people know about it. If this causes him to cry, do not worry. He needs to hear that you care that he is hurting. It helps him learn that tears are acceptable. He will soon return to the day's activities.

Effects on the child

Emotional

Matthew may experience mood swings of high excitement and total withdrawal. He may cry over small things and may display regressive behaviour – thumb sucking, rocking or wanting to be close to adults. He may be anxious at home time that those caring for him might forget him. Reassurance is the key here.

Be patient. Acknowledge that he is very sad and that his mum won't be coming back. He may ask for facts about Heaven or how it feels to be dead. He may talk of running into the road or cutting himself. There is an objective fascination about death as well as a subjective loss and fear.

Educational

He will tend to lose ground in what he has recently learnt. His concentration span will be short and he will be easily distracted. His drawings and stories may have a predominance of death in them – a normal outworking of grief.

Make sure you correct any misinformation. If Grandma has told him Mum has turned into a star or is now an angel holding his hand as he crosses the road, should you contradict her fantasy? Children need concrete facts. Tell him what you believe and admit that Grandma may believe something else. Teach the whole class what stars are made of and point out that real, warm hands need to be held when crossing the road.

I recall one of my social work students coming back horrified from a visit to a 4-year-old. He was alone in the house, his single parent mum having gone to work, but he assured the social worker that Granny was looking after him. When she insisted on meeting Granny she was faced with an urn full of ashes on the mantlepiece. His mum's departing remark was always, 'Granny will look after you' and he had complete faith that he was safe in her care!

In the long term, Matthew may fall behind while he adjusts to the social changes at home. He will thrive on being encouraged, even when making quite small progress, and he will need to know that it takes a long time to get over a major death.

Behavioural

He may well attention-seek. Try to ignore the bad and involve him in helping other children and adults. He needs to discover that his mum's death was not his fault. Sadly, children are often told, 'You'll be the death of me,' or, 'I'll kill you if you say that again!' It's not surprising that children equate death with something that they have done wrong. They might wish the substitute carer dead so their real mum will return, and they might try to make it happen by behaving badly.

A few kind glances and admitting, 'I know you're unhappy' are helpful. Eventually he may settle into a routine, but slip back into grief at holiday times or religious festivals. If he clings to you as a surrogate mother, make sure he spends time with other adults. He may show aggression to others. Help him to realize the anger inside him and to redirect it in sport or other constructive activities, rather than thumping his classmates.

Older children

The older child (aged 9 and above) stands more of a chance of being included in the family discussions about the funeral plans simply because he is more used to demanding his rights or being included. The child who is excluded at this stage will feel either that he is being blamed for the death or that the procedures are far more horrific than they really are. Children are used to being blamed for things to which they have not actually contributed, such as doors banging when Mother has a headache or when a parent storms off in a huff. 'Look what you've done now' rarely has an explanation behind it and the bewildered child will just assume guilt because an adult has apportioned it to him.

Thus, when a death occurs, the child naturally will think about the wrong that he did to the deceased and assume that to have caused the death. It is rare for a child to voice this guilt again since his natural defence is not to admit it, fearing retribution. The school has a particularly important task to play here, explaining that death is caused by something pretty big and not by an act of omission or commission by a small child.

An example of this is a family I visited recently. Five boys aged between 3 and 19 had just lost their father through a heart attack. The 9-year-old had been truanting from school and his father was walking with him to ensure that he got there. That child felt convinced that if Dad had not been taking him to school he would not have fallen in the street and died. I gently explained that wherever his father had been going on that day, the death would have happened and was then able to reassure the boy that he had acted very wisely by running to the Fire Station to get help. He could not have chosen to go to a more appropriate place.

Of course his guilt about truanting is still there, but it was important to separate the two issues in his mind. It was perhaps a little immoral of me to use the fact that it was his dad's wish that he should get back to school. I said this to the boy just at the point that they were all returning to school after the funeral, so I justified this little shove from behind. Were I to be using such tactics 6 or 12 months on, I would definitely have got a negative reaction. By then, anger, which is a natural part of bereavement, would be being experienced and such a remark would likely be met with the retort, 'If he wanted me to go to school, why did he go and die?' The issue of misusing our influence when children are so vulnerable must be watched.

I sometimes counsel those who recount remarks made to them at such times and they are indelibly imprinted on their minds and have often caused years of anguish. Adults with strong religious convictions need to be reminded not to misuse their zeal by suggesting that, for example, 'If you turn to Jesus, you can be sure of going to Heaven to be with Granny.' The child's acceptance of religion into their lives must be a real free-will choice, and not a means of gaining temporary comfort in hoping to see their loved ones again.

Explaining the reality

Fantasy is far more frightening than reality, and a child who is told that he cannot see his dead relative or would find the funeral too upsetting will find his mind running wild, off into the realms of horror films. While it is not easy to take a child to see a deceased relative or loved one before they are buried or cremated, it can be a valuable reassurance that death has occurred.

Being buried alive is a common childhood nightmare, and sadly often depicted in films. It has been estimated that by the age of about 10 a child will have witnessed 10,000 deaths on TV. I don't know how accurate that figure is, but your own observations will show you that in any one week, news broadcasts, TV dramas, plus a few action movies can soon accumulate a score. What the child rarely sees is the impact of the death on the family and wider community of the individual, and how they respond to it. Frequently, children are confused when the hero leaps from the tenth floor of a flaming building and survives but the bad guy does not. This just reinforces the myth which says, 'Bad people die, good ones don't.' When that is compounded by our tradition which says one must not speak ill of the dead, the confusion in the mind of a child becomes very great.

The class could debate the various ways in which sadness is expressed by humans, whether animals experience it, and what society does with it. Such opportunities taken in context are very enriching, but the teacher must be prepared to acknowledge his or her own sadness too.

The child may have heard talk of a wake or social gathering after the funeral and be totally confused as to what it is. If he registers that there is food around, he may wonder why he is being excluded from the party.

Explanations are needed. Yes, the dead person is in a coffin. It will be put in the earth or the curtains will be drawn round before it goes in to be burnt. In giving the child a choice he needs to know what he is actually opting in or out of.

Seeing adults cry, while distressing, assures the child that sadness affects everyone. If small children are attending, it is a good idea that they are seated with an adult who can explain what is happening. This should be someone who is close to the child but not as directly affected as the parents, so they can concentrate on the service and their own grief and not feel their child-care duties at that moment.

One family stopped in the middle of burying the ashes of their 1-year-old because his 10-year-old sister insisted on writing a poem to be buried under the rose tree among the ashes. It seemed almost farcical when the girl twice ran into the garden to ask how to spell 'remembered' and what rhymed with 'everlasting'. But the family waited patiently. Later, the girl's teacher was able to use the opportunity to have a classroom discussion about the different ways that sadness can be expressed in humans.

It is imperative that children be given the choice about whether or not to go to the funeral. If they prefer to come to school, they may need space at the time of the funeral to do their own joining in – perhaps reading quietly or going to the sick room.

Before they decide whether to attend the funeral an adult should explain that funerals generally have a few prayers and two hymns, and that the service usually lasts no more than 30 minutes; this will be useful information they may not get elsewhere.

The effects of bereavement on learning

In the early months following a family bereavement, the child will be preoccupied and his academic work may suffer. As it does so, he should be told that it is not his fault and just be encouraged to do his best. Because the concentration span is diminished, it may be possible to break up the time that the child is required to work. For example, while doing some written work it could be suggested that he goes to the library to find a book on the subject and then returns to work. So that the child does not stand out as being different, send three others to do the same. Alternatively, suggest that an illustration or some craft work should divide up the concentration time.

Strong, irrational outbursts of emotion may be experienced, and the child and his classmates will not naturally equate these with bereavement. It is helpful to tell the child that while he is sad he will find himself short-tempered. Diverting his attention by running an errand for you or giving him a chance to explain how he feels inside can really help.

Social effects

Bereavements may last a long time. For adults it is often two to three years before they are able to focus on the future rather than the past. Children will oscillate between getting on with the here and now and lapsing into periods of mourning. This is especially the case if their family circumstances change. For example, they may move to live with an aunt, or Father may take in a girlfriend. The child will need to test out these new relationships, usually by being as beastly as possible, to see if they will go away.

When a child loses a sibling, the parents may frequently glorify the dead child and be quite brusque with the others, or alternatively may be over-protective. Either way the child will experience unsettling changes in familial relationships and he may react aggressively towards all adults as a result.

The school must remember that it is providing the greatest stability in the child's life and therefore he needs consistent and firm handling, with an acknowledgement that you understand some of his churned up feelings, and in due time he will feel better. Few adults understand the feelings which can flood over them, so it can be assumed that children do not and they need to be encouraged that it is a normal process and it will eventually pass.

Anniversaries can be difficult times too. In the first year after a death there will be many of these. The first birthday and Christmas without the loved one, Easter and Mother's Day are often extra painful, and then there is the death day one year on. Be ready for the child to find these problematic and let him talk about how he feels. The anniversary of the death day is particularly difficult since there is no longer the original shock to buffer them and they sometimes find the pain of reliving it all again very hard. For example, if little brother was killed on the way to school, one year on his older siblings will be thinking, 'This time last year we were just walking along the path together and then there was the squeal of the brakes of the bus and...' Such remembering projects them backwards into the very moment of death and it can be quite traumatic. You cannot be expected to note when each anniversary is, but listen carefully and the child will tell you.

Children sometimes appear to be intrigued by or preoccupied with death when there has been no apparent bereavement. All behaviour is meaningful, but finding its meaning is sometimes problematic. Talk to the child's parents and ask them if there has been a significant loss in the family. It might be an uncle whom the child barely knew, or it might be that there have been several deaths of elderly neighbours close by. The family may have dismissed the impact on the child, but if such deaths coincide with the child's inquisitiveness about death its significance can be important.

One child of 8 drew nothing but crashing planes and sea-monsters which ate people. The child had no respect for women in authority in the school, but he would be better behaved in the presence of the headmaster. His father had died of a heart attack two weeks before the boy started school, but it was only when he was under pressure to begin to perform that his grief really showed itself.

I discovered that the mother had given in to him, an only child, since his father's death and he had become the dictator in the house, choosing what they would eat and when he would go to bed. The mother had no control over him, since the father had really been the key figure in raising the child. Clearly the school had to exert authority over this very little boy who had become a big presence. He wavered in his perception of himself, between the 'little boy who hasn't got a daddy' and 'the man of the house – if I want to watch TV 'til midnight, I can.' This child was frightening himself since he could not really find out who he was or how old he was expected to behave.

His mother, teacher and I worked out a strategy of being firm over things which must be obeyed, with sanctions which were carried out, and encouraging him to have friends round to play so that he spent less leisure time in the presence of adults. I asked his mother to allow or even encourage some more babyish, silly behaviour in an appropriate context. Our rationale was to give him back his childhood while placing expectations on him appropriate to an 8-year-old. We also organized some play therapy, since he had never been given an explanation of his father's sudden death.

Children frequently have a deep attachment to a family pet and when that dies they can be devastated. It should not be underestimated how deeply the loss of a dog or cat can affect the child, especially if it has lived in the family since they were born. In times of sadness, children may have been used to taking the cat to bed with them for solace, so when the cat dies there is a dual blow. Parents will often dismiss the grief over animals as silly and sentimental and the child will be left feeling that they are mourning inappropriately. Please assure them that they are not.

Before closing this section on the individual child's grief and the part school can play in it, I should deal with the issue of single parents. A child who has two parents, one of whom dies, will be understandably terrified about how they will manage if the remaining one dies. This of course applies when parents split up, too.

Children will see through the false reassurances which tell them that the parent with whom they live will never die on them. What they need to know is who they should turn to if it did happen. Often there will be a logical surrogate family, but a proper emergency plan should be laid down with phone numbers and clear instructions about who to ring.

The remaining parent is unlikely to be bold enough to raise this issue, but if possible the school should suggest it to the bereaved parent.

If a child has grown up in a single parent family, there are added problems when death occurs. If a sibling has died, the parent will have a tendency to reject the other children while they yearn for the lost one. This may leave the child in your class contemplating death himself in order to gain his parent's approval. When there are two parents, there is a greater chance that the child may experience some positive regard.

In a single parent family, the parent's ability to care, even at a basic level, is sometimes lessened because they have no adult to comfort them or to share the domestic tasks. When a single parent dies, there is an immediate disruption to the child's life, since he must be found a new home and a surrogate parent, and may even be split up from his siblings. It must not be underestimated how such disruption will add to the child's sense of loss.

It is difficult enough for a child to cope with his grief in the privacy of his own home, but trying to do so while settling into a foster home or not being able to care for his siblings is horrific, and such situations will reverberate in the classroom for many months.

Since our society has moved towards a situation where fewer adults marry or provide a permanent coupling for the duration of the child's life, with some single parents preferring to bring up children alone, we can only expect that there will be greater challenges. When a parent dies and a new liaison is formed which may be transitory, the child will vent his anger on the interloper causing conflict for his natural parent. The teacher can help by explaining that adults need companionship and comfort, and reassuring the child that their lost one is of no less importance and has not been replaced.

The mother of an 8-year-old whose father died last year admitted to me that she felt quite murderous toward her daughter who rudely shouted at a visiting male friend, 'You're not going to take my mummy out, you're not my daddy, I hate you!' And with that she kicked him. This atypical behaviour descended into a screaming match all round. The mother feared it would destroy the tentative new friendship.

I helped her to stand in her daughter's shoes, to understand her fear that she might go off with this man and leave the children. There was anger that her father wasn't there and was being usurped by someone she did not know, and a subconscious awareness that another man in the house might mean that they all had to go through the terrible trauma all over again. Once the mother could step outside her own sadness and look from the child's perspective, the behaviour seemed slightly more acceptable and she could discuss how she could handle any recurrence better next time.

The teacher is frequently seen as a wise counsellor by the parent who may accept what you say knowing that you have the children's best interests at heart. Looking at any situation from a different perspective is always valuable, but try to recognize and acknowledge the parent's hurt too. It's a bit like holding up two mirrors; if you only take the child's viewpoint you may alienate the parent.

The time when this kind of help is most needed is often many months into the bereavement. The parent may be at a parents' evening and share their despair at the behaviour and educational decline in their children. Check up on the length of bereavement time and let them know that your pupil is experiencing very much the same inner turmoil and powerful emotions that they are, while also struggling to keep up with the class. Time will lessen the degree of disruption, but one is always aware that if a child falls too far behind educationally he may never catch up. Your reassurance that the school is monitoring the slip-back and will help to organize extra tuition or counselling, or that you know that the child has the capability to bounce back when he is more stable, must be realistically founded.

The parent may not be aware that the bereavement is still taking its toll. I was once a school governor, and the school concerned would refer such children to me for a few reflective sessions. You may also have contact with a counsellor whose help you could offer. There are some useful books listed in the 'Recommended reading and resources' at the end of this book.

Spiritual and cultural issues

Spiritual issues are governed by the teacher's perspective and by the family's background. Some teachers, for instance, will have a strong belief system. However, try to respect the beliefs of the child and their family and avoid imposing your own views.

Other teachers will share with the children their own doubts about the mystery of life and death and teach children about the diverse range of beliefs held. Children have inquisitive minds and may well be keen to conduct a mini-survey of all the adults in the school or some members of their family to discover what others believe and so begin to discover their own belief system.

Children aged 4 and over can be taught that most religions believe that there is a part of us that lives on after death, but which takes different forms. They could be taught at an appropriate time of the year, to tie in with significant dates in the calendar, or religious festivals.

You can also take the opportunity to have general discussions about faith and death – for example, how can there be a benevolent God or deity who tolerates death and pain?

Spiritual and cultural issues need explaining

You will need to address cultural and spiritual issues together. Some children are caught in a cross-cultural situation. They have been born in this country and have an understanding of the common social conventions when someone dies. Their parents, on the other hand, may have strong links with a culture that the child knows little about. Death brings cultural roots to the surface. A Hindu family which has emigrated from India may impoverish itself in order to fly a body back to India or send someone with ashes to scatter on the Ganges. The importance of this act to the family may be lost on the young child and add to the mythology and confusion.

Children from minority ethnic families may notice that mourners tend to wear black in Europe and white in Asia. They may be confused if the school is arranging for boys and girls to attend the funeral if their own culture only permits men to attend (this is the case in some Muslim and Sikh traditions, for example). Be careful to take account of different religious practices before you suggest that the whole class might attend a funeral. Some faiths, such as Islam and Sikhism, require that the body is buried within 24 hours of death, so there will not be time to help the children to participate. You may be able to suggest a memorial service in the school instead.

If your school is within a multi-faith area, why not ask some representatives from the various faiths to come in and explain their culture and belief systems surrounding death? This could be done as a community link for the school and as a way of adding to the children's religious education classes.

Where I live we tend to be faced primarily with children from a secular background who are suddenly projected into Christianity for a few brief weeks when someone dies, so God and Heaven become linked with death rather than exasperated expletives! Multi-faith schools present plenty of opportunities for learning about different religious practices, but single-faith schools also have advantages in having a shared outlook which can also help to nurture an understanding and caring environment – the child's faith can be a source of comfort to them.

Summary

Our society is afraid of death and tends to push it away, yet grief needs to be expressed in order to be understood. Young children live more in the present than adults do, and they seem to get over a death more quickly. Periodically, though, they will have times of grieving.

Teaching on death and dying should be an important part of the school curriculum. The importance of teaching about new life has long been recognized. Twenty years ago, schools were inviting the school nurse in to show how a nappy was changed. Today, if a staff member has a baby she is often asked to bring her baby back as a teaching aid and may well feel able to breastfeed the infant in the children's presence as part of their learning. Learning about death is equally important.

I trust that you will feel able to try out some of the ideas suggested in this short book. You will be breaking new ground. It will not necessarily be comfortable or acceptable to those around you, but be encouraged – facing the concept and mythology of death and its surrounding practices with young children will fit them for life when it is done in context. Perhaps, when they are adult, they may feel able to share ideas and beliefs more freely than your generation has been able to do. Then you will have taught both the facts of life and death in a rounded way and equipped your pupils to one day face their own mortality in a way that is based on a firmer footing than traditional folklore. Go to it, you can do it!

Recommended reading and resources

Recommended reading

For children aged 7 to 11 years

Edwards, N. (2003) Four books: *Saying Goodbye – To a Parent; To a Grandparent; To a Brother or Sister; To a Friend.* London: Chrysalis Children's Books for the Child Bereavement Trust.

Stickney, D. (2007) *Waterbugs and Dragonflies.* London: Continuum.

Varley, S. (1994) *Badger's Parting Gifts.* New York: Mulberry Books.

For professionals and parents

Di Ciacco, J.A. (2008) *The Colors of Grief: Understanding a Child's Journey through Loss from Birth to Adulthood.* London: Jessica Kingsley Publishers.

Dyregrov, A. (2008) *Grief in Children: A Handbook for Adults,* 2nd edn. London: Jessica Kingsley Publishers.

Goldman, L. (2006) *Children Also Grieve: Talking about Death and Healing.* London: Jessica Kingsley Publishers.

Goldman, L. (2009) *Great Answers to Difficult Questions about Death: What Children Need to Know.* London: Jessica Kingsley Publishers.

Kubler-Ross, E. (2008) *On Life After Death.* Berkeley, CA: Celestial Arts.

Smith, S.C. and Pennells, M. (eds) (1995) *Interventions with Bereaved Children.* London: Jessica Kingsley Publishers.

Sorensen, J. (2008) *Overcoming Loss: Activities and Stories to Help Transform Children's Grief and Loss.* London: Jessica Kingsley Publishers.

Ward. B. (1995) *Good Grief: Exploring Feelings, Loss and Death with Under Elevens* (2nd edition). London: Jessica Kingsley Publishers.

Wells, R. (2007) *Helping Children Cope with Grief* (new edition). London: Sheldon Press.

Useful organizations and websites

Australian Child and Adolescent Trauma, Loss and Grief Network (ACATLGN)

www.earlytraumagrief.anu.edu.au

The Australian Child and Adolescent, Trauma, Loss and Grief Network links parents, members of the community and professionals and encourages them to share experiences and resources on the care of children and youth experiencing the impact of trauma, loss and grief.

BBC Health: Helping Bereaved Children

www.bbc.co.uk/health/bereavement/psych-help-children. shtml

A factsheet with important tips on how you can help children overcome the problems they may face when they have lost someone close to them.

The Child Bereavement Trust

www.childbereavement.org.uk

The Child Bereavement Trust has, over many years, developed a list of books and resources which others have found helpful.

Childhood Bereavement Network

www.ncb.org.uk/cbn

An organization that aims to improve the access of bereaved children and young people to information, guidance and support.

Cruse Bereavement Care

www.crusebereavementcare.org.uk

As well as providing free care to all bereaved people, the charity also offers information, support and training services to those who are looking after them.

The Dougy Center: The National Center for Grieving Children and Families

www.dougy.org

A US-based organization that provides support and training locally, nationally and internationally to individuals and organizations seeking to assist children in grief.

The Grief Encounter Project

www.griefencounter.org.uk

The Grief Encounter Project is a Bereavement Charity set up to help bereaved children and their families.

Jigsaw4u

www.jigsaw4u.org.uk

To support children and young people, and their families, who have experienced loss and trauma and to empower them to have a voice in decision making about their lives.

National Network for Child Care

www.nncc.org/Guidance/understand.death.html

A useful factsheet called 'Learning to Live Through Loss: Helping Children Understand Death'.

RD4U

www.rd4u.org.uk

Part of Cruse Bereavement Care's Youth Involvement Project, RD4U is a website designed for young people by young people to support them after the death of someone close.

Winston's Wish

www.winstonswish.org.uk

Winston's Wish is the leading childhood bereavement charity and the largest provider of services to bereaved children, young people and their families in the UK.

CD/audio tape

When Grief Comes to School by Ann Chadwick

An expanded version of this book with examples of how to help and ideas for classroom work. Available from Anchor Recordings at http://shopping.anchor-recordings.com.

Children Also Grieve
Talking about Death and Healing
Linda Goldman

Children Also Grieve is an imaginative resource, fully illustrated with color photographs, that offers support and reassurance to children coming to terms with the loss of a close friend or relative and to adults who are supporting them through their bereavement.

Hardback: £16.99 / $22.95
ISBN 978 1 84310 808 5

The first part of the book is designed to be read and worked through by children. The story tells of the experiences of Henry, the dog of a family whose grandfather has died. During Henry's progress through the different stages of bereavement, he learns strategies for coping with his grief. At various stages of the story, Goldman provides readers with the opportunity to share their own reactions to loss through words and pictures, using specific prompt questions that encourage the exploration of different facets of grief.

The second part includes a list of useful vocabulary to help children express their feelings about bereavement, a bibliography of other useful resources for both children and adults, and a section that will help adults to understand and aid children throughout the grief process. This last section also explains the approach taken in the story, details typical responses to bereavement, and discusses useful ways in which adults can discuss and share grief with children.

This book is an invaluable tool for bereaved children and those who care for them.

Talking with Children and Young People about Death and Dying
2nd edition
Mary Turner
Illustrated by Bob Thomas

Talking with Children and Young People about Death and Dying is a popular resource designed to help adults talk to bereaved children and young people.

Mary Turner explains the various aspects and stages of bereavement and offers useful insights into the concerns of children experiencing grief or facing an imminent bereavement. She addresses children's common fears and worries, dreams and nightmares, and acknowledges the effect of trauma on the grief process. This second edition includes a new section for adults on understanding the distress of a bereaved child and also a list of useful contacts.

It is a fully photocopiable workbook that enables adults to deal with these issues sensitively and explains, for example, how to choose appropriate words to support the child. It will empower and equip adults working with bereaved children to encourage them to communicate their pain and understand the often contradictory emotions aroused by the death of someone close to them.

Paperback: £19.99 / $36.95
ISBN 978 1 84310 441 4

Grief in Young Children
A Handbook for Adults
Atle Dyregrov
Foreword by Professor William Yule

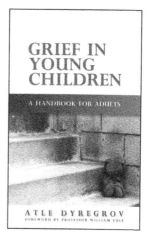

Paperback: £9.99 / $18.95
ISBN 978 1 84310 650 0

It is a common misconception that pre-school children are not capable of experiencing grief in the same way that older children do. *Grief in Young Children* challenges this assumption, demonstrating that although young children may not express grief in the same way as older children, they still need to be supported through loss.

Illustrated throughout with case examples, the author explores young children's reactions to death and loss, both immediately after the event and over time. For example, young children may engage in `magic thinking', believing that wishing that someone were dead can actually cause death, which leads to feelings of guilt.

Full of practical advice on issues such as how to keep children in touch with their memories, answer their questions, allay their fears and explore their feelings through play, this accessible book enables adults to work with children to develop an acceptance of grief and an understanding of death and loss.

Grief in Children

A Handbook for Adults

2nd edition

Atle Dyregrov

Foreword by Professor
William Yule

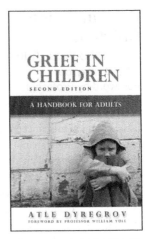

This fully updated second edition
of *Grief in Children* provides an
accessible overview of children's
understanding of death at different
ages and gives a detailed outline
of exactly how the adults around
them can best help them cope.

Whether a child experiences
the death of a parent, sibling,
other relation or friend, or of a
classmate or teacher, it is important

Paperback: £14.99 / $24.95
ISBN 978 1 84310 612 8

for those caring for bereaved children to know how to respond
appropriately to the child's needs. This book deals with a range
of common physical and psychological responses and describes
the methods of approaching grief in children that have been
shown to work best. The author provides guidance on how loss
and bereavement should be handled at school, explains when it
is appropriate to involve expert professional help and discusses
the value of bereavement groups for children and support for
caregivers.

Illustrated with case studies and incorporating current research,
this book is essential reading for parents, carers, counsellors,
teachers and all those concerned with the welfare of bereaved
children.

CPI Antony Rowe
Eastbourne, UK
April 04, 2025